Florence + the Machine
CEREMONIALS

12. JUL.

C015009850

D1514268

Wise Publications
PART OF THE MUSIC SALES GROUP

LONDON / NEW YORK / PARIS / SYDNEY / COPENHAGEN / BERLIN / MADRID / HONG KONG / TOKYO

PUBLISHED BY
WISE PUBLICATIONS
14-15 BERNERS STREET, LONDON W1T 3LJ, UK.

EXCLUSIVE DISTRIBUTORS:
MUSIC SALES LIMITED
DISTRIBUTION CENTRE, NEWMARKET ROAD,
BURY ST EDMUNDS, SUFFOLK IP33 3YB, UK.
MUSIC SALES PTY LIMITED
20 RESOLUTION DRIVE, CARINGBAH,
NSW 2229, AUSTRALIA.

ORDER NO. AM1004344
ISBN: 978-1-78038-406-1
THIS BOOK © COPYRIGHT 2011 WISE PUBLICATIONS,
A DIVISION OF MUSIC SALES LIMITED.

EDITED BY JENNI NOREY.
MUSIC ARRANGED BY DEREK JONES.
MUSIC PROCESSED BY PAUL EWERS MUSIC DESIGN.

PRINTED IN THE EU.

YOUR GUARANTEE OF QUALITY:

AS PUBLISHERS, WE STRIVE TO PRODUCE EVERY
BOOK TO THE HIGHEST COMMERCIAL STANDARDS.

THIS BOOK HAS BEEN CAREFULLY DESIGNED TO MINIMISE AWKWARD
PAGE TURNS AND TO MAKE PLAYING FROM IT A REAL PLEASURE.

PARTICULAR CARE HAS BEEN GIVEN TO SPECIFYING ACID-FREE, NEUTRAL-SIZED PAPER
MADE FROM PULPS WHICH HAVE NOT BEEN ELEMENTAL CHLORINE BLEACHED.

THIS PULP IS FROM FARMED SUSTAINABLE FORESTS AND
WAS PRODUCED WITH SPECIAL REGARD FOR THE ENVIRONMENT.

THROUGHOUT, THE PRINTING AND BINDING HAVE BEEN PLANNED TO ENSURE A STURDY,
ATTRACTIVE PUBLICATION WHICH SHOULD GIVE YEARS OF ENJOYMENT.

IF YOUR COPY FAILS TO MEET OUR HIGH STANDARDS,
PLEASE INFORM US AND WE WILL GLADLY REPLACE IT.

WWW.MUSICSALES.COM

ONLY IF FOR A NIGHT

Words & Music by Paul Epworth & Florence Welch

4

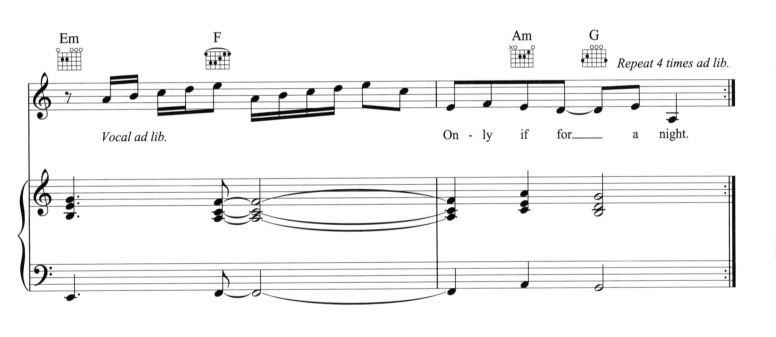

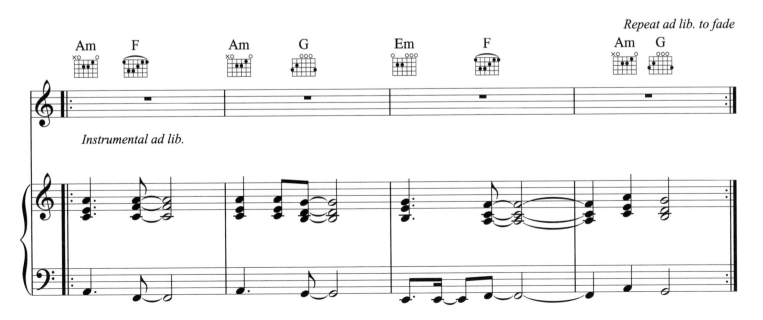

7

SHAKE IT OUT

Words & Music by Paul Epworth, Florence Welch
& Tom Hull

Re - grets col - lect_____ like old friends, here to re - live_____

_____ your dark - est mo - ments. I can see no way, I can see no way._____

And all of the ghouls_____ come out to play. And ev - er - y de - mon wants his pound of

flesh, but I like to keep____ some things to my - self.____ I like to keep____ my is - sues strong.____ It's al - ways dark - est be - fore the dawn.____ And I've been a fool____ and I've been blind.__ I can nev - er leave the past be - hind. I can see no way, I can see no way.__ I'm al - ways drag - ging that horse a - round.__

9

11

It's a fine ro - mance,_____ but it's left me so emp - ty. (Shake it off.)_

It's al - ways dark - est be - fore the dawn._____ (Oh, whoa,_

oh whoa.)_

And I'm damned if I___ do___ and I'm damned if I don't.___ So here's to drinks in the dark   at the

Shake it out, shake it out,____ shake it out, shake it out,____ oh, whoa.____

Shake it out, shake it out,____ shake it out, shake it out,____ oh, whoa.____

And it's hard to dance____ with a dev - il on your back.____ So shake him off,____

oh, whoa.____

14

Ooh,_____ ooh,_____ ooh,_____ ooh._____

Ooh,_____ ooh,_____ ooh,_____ ooh._____

Ooh,_____ ooh,_____ ooh,_____ ooh._____

Ooh,_____ ooh,_____ ooh,_____ ooh._____

WHAT THE WATER GAVE ME

Words & Music by Eg White & Florence Welch

1. Time, it took us to where the wat-
2. And oh, poor At- las, the world's a beast of a bur-

-er was. That's what the wat- er gave___ me. And
-den. You've been hold- ing on a long___ time. And

-turned them in ex-change for you. But would you have it an-y-oth-

-er way? Would you have it an-y oth-

-er way? You could-n't have it an-y-oth-er way.

'Cause she's a cru-el mis-tress and a

full of stones.___ Lay me down.___ Let the

on - ly sound___ be the o - ver -

- flow.___ So lay me

D.S. al Coda

Coda

- flow.___

Vocal ad lib.

21

NEVER LET ME GO

Words & Music by Paul Epworth, Florence Welch
& Tom Harpoon

breathe. No need to pray, no need to speak.

It seems a heav-y choice to make.

Now I'm un-der...

But now I am un-der...

Oh,__ and it's break-ing o-ver me,__

__ thou-sand miles__ down to__ the sea bed. Found the place__ to rest__ my

head. (Nev-er let me go. Nev-er let me go.)__ (Nev-er let me go. Nev-er let me go.)__ And the

arms of the o-cean are car-ry-ing__ me.__ And all this de-vo-tion was__

25

28

BREAKING DOWN

Words & Music by Florence Welch & James Ford

1. All a-lone. It was al-ways there, you see.

2. All a-lone. E-ven when I was a child,

30

LOVER TO LOVER

Words & Music by Florence Welch & Francis Eg White

NO LIGHT, NO LIGHT

Words & Music by Florence Welch & Isabella Summers

si-lence in be-tween___ what I thought and what I said. You are the

night time fear. You are the morn-ing when it's clear. When it's o - ver you're the start.___

___ You're___ my head and you're___ my heart. No light,___

___ no light___ in your bright___ blue eyes.___ I nev-er knew day-light___ could be so

42

43

44

SEVEN DEVILS

Words & Music by Paul Epworth & Florence Welch

49

lakes_____ can put the fire out. I'm gon-na raise the stakes._

I'm gon-na smoke you out. Sev-en dev-ils all a - round you.

Sev - en dev - ils in my___ house._____ See, they were there when I woke

up this morn - ing, I'll be dead be - fore the day is done.

Sev - en dev - ils all a - round you. Sev - en dev - ils in your_

_ house._____ See, I was dead when I woke up this morn -

-ing and I'll be dead be - fore the day is done._____

Be - fore the

HEARTLINES

Words & Music by Paul Epworth & Florence Welch

(Yeah.)_____ (Yeah.)_____ (Yeah.)_____

(Yeah.)_____ (Yeah.)_____ (Yeah.)_____

8vb throughout

1. Oh, the riv - er, oh, the riv - er, it's run-ing free.___ And oh, the joy,___ oh, the joy
2. On the sea___ and on the sea___ and land o - ver land.___ Creep-ing and a crawl-ing like the

it brings to me.___ But I know it 'll have to drown me be-
sea o - ver sand.___ Still I fol - low heart - lines on your hand.___

SPECTRUM

Words & Music by Paul Epworth & Florence Welch

All This And Heaven Too

Words & Music by Florence Welch & Isabella Summers

-ing. All this heav-en___ nev-er___ ___ could de-scribe such a feel-ing as I'm heal-ing.

Words were nev-er___ so use-ful,___ so I was scream-ing out a lan-guage___ that I nev-er knew ex-ist-ed be-fore.___

LEAVE MY BODY

Words & Music by Paul Epworth, Florence Welch
& Tom Harpoon

123456789